MORE THAN
CANDLELIGHTING

MORE THAN CANDLELIGHTING

A Guide for Training Acolytes

by PHILIP C. PEACE

THE PILGRIM PRESS
NEW YORK

Library of Congress Cataloging in Publication Data

Peace, Philip C., 1930–
  More than candlelighting.

  1. Acolytes—Handbooks, manuals, etc. I. Title.
BV195.5.P4   1983   264   82-18973
ISBN 0-8298-0642-3 (pbk.)

Biblical quotations are from the *Revised Standard Version of the Bible*, copyright 1946, 1952 and © 1971 by the Division of Christian Education, National Council of Churches, and are used by permission.

All photographs were taken at Shepherd of the Hills United Methodist Church, Mission Viejo, California, where the author is senior pastor. Photographs by Dave Lindahl.

The Pilgrim Press, 132 West 31 Street, New York, NY 10001

Table of Contents

Introduction

A top priority of every church is establishing and maintaining an effective program of Christian education for boys and girls. But how many programs are there today that provide not only Christian education but also an opportunity for service to the church, stimulation for possible church-related occupations later on, and the rare opportunity for pastor and youth to relate to each other on a regular basis?

There is such a program so attractive to pre-teen youngsters that they participate enthusiastically. I am referring to the unique Christian education/experiential program with which this book deals—a well-planned, comprehensive program for *acolytes*. Such a program can be one of the most satisfying and productive experiences a busy pastor could hope for. It involves the pastor and a group of young people on a weekly basis for several months, or even years—but nowhere else could a pastor better spend his or her time than with a group of impressionable young people in the church, dealing with the basics, and establishing close personal relationships as well. How many pastors can claim to be on a first-name basis with thirty or more young people between the ages of eight and twelve? This is one of the many benefits of such a program. But the greatest benefit of all is that the program serves as an ideal vehicle for the faith development of youth. This is a good opportunity for the pastor, church members, and parents positively to affect the lives of youth while being enriched themselves.

Carl Ward, in an article in *Music Ministry*, sums it up this way: "The acolyte program exposes a [person] at his [or her] most impressionable age to the very heart of the church's worship. What could be a greater blessing than to develop this acolyte program throughout the church to give dignity and meaning to the service of worship and to inspire young [people] to dedicate their lives to the service of Christ and the Church."

The program outlined in this book is the result of some twenty years of experience with acolytes and of sharing programs and ideas gathered from various churches, pastors, and lay people who have ministered in this area. The course also reflects research in various areas that make up the acolyte curriculum.

CHAPTER 1

Acolytes Viewed Historically

The practice for which the modern-day acolyte is best known—the lighting of candles on the altar—came into prominence about the ninth century, when large candlesticks were carried by the acolytes and placed on the floor of the sanctuary near the altar. Gradually the candlesticks began to appear on the altar itself. Because of the added height, a candlelighter was developed to reach the top of the candles and to provide a decorative container for the tapers carried in the processional.

But let's take an imaginary trip back in time to the year A.D. 525. We are in the magnificent city of Rome. It is Sunday, and we have joined the throngs of worshipers in the splendid cathedral for high mass. There is an air of excitement. Before the mass starts, there is an impressive processional down the long aisle. Twelve young men dressed in colorful vestments lead the way for the bishop and priests. A stranger might be curious about the large number of youth in the processional and wonder what their role will be in the mass. The stranger would soon learn that these are acolytes who have a very important function in the mass and other public services in the ancient church. Two acolytes lead the processional. One is the crucifer, who carries the large iron cross called the crucifix. The other carries the censer suspended by a chain. As he swings it gently back and forth, fragrant clouds of smoke billowing from burning incense signal the arrival of the sacred ministers. A third acolyte carries the lavabo bowl, in which the bishop washes his hands before consecrating the bread. Attention is soon focused on one acolyte moving very cautiously, for he holds the precious chalice of silver and gold in which the wine is consecrated. Still another acolyte carries the chrism, consecrated oil used by the bishop in baptism and confirmation. Once the mass begins, the acolytes have duties to perform in assisting the bishop and priests. Several acolytes have the responsibility of carrying lighted tapers to provide illumination for the various parts of the mass, for example, when the scripture is read. Likewise, as the bishop and priests administer the sacrament to the communicants, acolytes provide the necessary lighting.

At the conclusion of the mass, the acolytes perform one of their most important duties: They reverently place the remaining consecrated bread into cloth bags and carry the sacrament to the sick and those unable to attend mass, sometimes even the faithful who are imprisoned because of religious persecution. (This practice symbolized the unity of the church even though the faithful were scattered in many places.)

If the stranger were curious enough to inquire, he might learn that the acolytes had many other duties in addition to assisting at the mass and at other worship services. The acolyte was the bishop's aide, his "right-hand man." He accompanied the bishop on his journeys and visitations. When the bishop had messages or correspondence to deliver, the acolytes carried the mail.

The acolyte is well named. The word acolyte comes from the Greek *akolouthos*, meaning follower, attendant, one who serves, assists, or helps.

In A.D. 251, "Cornelius, the Bishop of Rome, sent a letter to Bishop Fabius of Antioch saying that at that time there were forty-two acolytes in Rome."[*] The office of the acolyte grew to be one of great respect and importance, and by the sixth century, when we make our imaginary visit, the office was considered vital enough that it required ordination, after a period of instruction by the bishop. "At his 'ordination' or admission to the order, the acolyte was handed a candle by the arch-deacon to show that the church would be in his care."[†] In later years at the ordination ceremony, the bishop presented the candidate with an unlighted candle, a candlestick, and an empty cruet (a small glass vessel). These symbolized the principal duties of the acolyte: to light the candles on the altar, to carry candles in the procession, to prepare wine and water for the mass during the solemn singing of the Gospel, and generally to assist the clergy in the mass. In his instructions, the bishop reminded the candidate that he would do these duties only when he had offered himself as a "sacrifice to God" by a chaste life and good works. The bishop then prayed that God would grant the acolyte strength to do this.

---

[*]Calder Gibson, *Manual for Acolytes* (Philadelphia: Fortress Press, 1959), p. 4. © 1959 Calder A. Gibson, II.
[†]Ibid. (quoted from the Statua of Aries), p. 6.

CHAPTER 2

The Acolyte Viewed Locally

THE CONCEPT OF ACOLYTE MINISTRY

An interesting worship bulletin once crossed my desk. The names and titles of worship participants were listed on the back of the bulletin in this fashion (the names are fictitious):

Greeters:	Bill and Mary Jones
Child Care:	Joan Smith
Choir Director:	Harry Jackson
Organist:	Mary Adams
Minister:	Tom Black
Acolyte:	Good grief! Who knows?

The last line no doubt provoked a few chuckles, but it also conveyed the idea that acolytes are little more than ecclesiastical decoration, and irrelevant decoration at that. One might question the use of acolytes at all if their role is so insignificant in the average worship service. Such an attitude does a great disservice to the traditional concept of the office. More important, a great opportunity is missed if the acolyte is not fully utilized and the potential of the role appreciated.

Worship services are enhanced by well-trained acolytes. Acolytes, in turn, benefit from comprehensive instruction in Christian life and worship and from standards for qualification. Not many churches seem to avail themselves of this opportunity, as shown by a survey of 365 churches in Southern California. A doctoral research project of the Rev. James Oliver, the survey indicated that 70 percent of the churches polled used acolytes, but in the majority of those churches the acolytes did nothing more than light candles. Only 36 percent used acolytes to assist with the offering, the next most common duty they were assigned.

Historically, the office of acolyte was versatile and flexible (see chapter 1). This can still be true, although many of the functions carried out by acolytes in the early church are no longer needed. These pages describe many ways for acolytes to serve their church and God in a broad program that does not confine their task to lighting candles. The program suggested calls for a minimum of three months' training and instruction, which contains an incalculable bonus: The close association of pastor and young congregants over an extended period of time allows each to deal with the basics of Christian life, worship, and ministry and to know one another on a level deeper than otherwise possible.

THE DUTIES OF THE ACOLYTE
IN THE LOCAL CHURCH

Lighting the candles. Lighting and extinguishing the candles at the regular worship services and at special services—for example, weddings—are among the duties of modern-day acolytes. The use of the lighted candle is an adaptation of the practice of using oil lamps for light during biblical times. Candles were not in use prior to A.D. 100. Simply by a process of substitution, the candle began to be used as a symbol of Jesus Christ, the light of the world. Thus the lighted candles

on the altar remind us of the words of Jesus found in John 8:12 and 9:5: "I am the light of the world." The number of candles and their position on the altar may vary with individual churches. It is recommended that there be at least two for the celebration of Holy Communion, signifying the dual nature of Christ, divine and human.

Using more than two candles for services other than Holy Communion is a common practice. The larger number of candles is a throwback to traditional weekday nonliturgical services, consisting of Matins, Vespers, Lauds, and so on. The practice of placing three candles of equal height on either side of the crucifix or cross was fairly well established by the late Middle Ages. The number of acolytes used for lighting the candles may vary, but two is average. For a small chancel area, one acolyte will suffice.

When only two candles are on the altar, and two acolytes are employed, the following procedure is suggested: Assuming the acolytes process down the center aisle, let them ascend the steps together and each light one candle. By watching out of the corners of their eyes, they can coordinate their movements unobtrusively. When one candle lights ahead of the other, let that acolyte keep the candlelighter on the flame until the partner's candle lights. The acolytes then remove the candlelighters at the same time, turn to face each other, and extinguish the tapers simultaneously. In unison, the acolytes turn to the chancel area and walk to their seats, moving quietly and deliberately. If there are more than two candles, the Christ candles (those closest to the cross) should be lit first, then, moving outward from the cross, the others are lit in turn. This process symbolizes that light flows from Christ, "the light of the world," to the church. It is important to have the acolytes visually check that no flames have gone out while others were being lighted. *Caution:* Young acolytes should not be given the task of lighting the candlelighters. Arrange with ushers or other adults to be responsible for this task, and make sure that matches are not left in an accessible area.

In churches that have a processional, the acolytes should lead the way, preceding the choir and worship leaders. They go directly to the altar and light the candles as the choir and worship leaders take their places in the chancel. In some worship services, the acolytes light the candles at the start of the prelude. They then go to the narthex and join the choir for the processional. One of the acolytes may serve as the crucifer if a third acolyte is not available for that function (see "The processional," page 20). As an alternative, if there is no processional with the choir, the acolytes may process by themselves down the aisle. This offers more symbolism and dignity than if the acolytes merely enter casually from a side door and perform the simple candlelighting function that an usher could do with a match. When the acolytes process and recess down the aisle at the proper times, it calls attention to the symbolic meaning of Christ leading the church, which gathers to worship then scatters to serve (see "Extinguishing the candles," below).

The lighting of the candles may be listed as part of the order of service:

Organ Prelude
Lighting of the Candles
Call to Worship
Processional Hymn . . . etc.

Extinguishing the candles. Traditionally, the flames are extinguished while the congregation is singing the final hymn. Acolytes follow a procedure opposite to the opening sequence, that is, moving *toward* the cross. Before putting out the last flames (those of the Christ candles), the acolytes relight their tapers and prepare to recess. Carrying the flame back down the aisle symbolizes the movement of the faithful back into the world to serve. The church becomes "scattered" after having been the "gathered" community at worship.

The offering. When the offering is to be received, acolytes may take the offering plates or baskets to the ushers, perhaps

meeting them at the chancel rail. Here again it is important that their movements be deliberate and coordinated; they should turn to face each other, and be reseated in unison while the ushers pass the plates. When the ushers return to the rail, the acolytes receive the plates and either place them on the altar or present them to the pastor or other leader. (This may take place during the singing of the Doxology.) These procedures can be modified according to the particular ritual sequence of the individual church.

Holy Communion. When observing the sacrament of Holy Communion, the pastor should make a special effort to involve the acolytes. Experience has shown that youngsters find this service most meaningful and will naturally assume an attitude of reverence and respect. This is especially true if the pastor has included a session on the meaning of Holy Communion in the training classes. At that class, an explanatory "model" communion service helps prepare the acolytes spiritually as well as practically.

There are numerous possibilities for involving the acolytes, depending on the order of service and the physical characteristics of the chancel-sanctuary area. The following is one example: During the celebration of Holy Communion, one acolyte can collect the empty cups from the individual communicants in a container after each has communed. (This church communion rail has no built-in receptacles to receive the cups.) A second acolyte quietly receives the container of empty cups from the first acolyte and takes them to the sacristy, where a member of the altar guild is stationed during the service. This acolyte is also available to bring more elements to the pastor if needed. Other minor responsibilities include the placement and removal of a partition in the altar rail (used only during administration of communion) at the proper moment, and having the neck microphone ready for use by the pastor in the sanctuary area as he or she faces the altar for communion prayers. All this is done with dignity and decorum.

Pew communion also provides opportunities for acolyte participation. The pastor will judge how to use the acolytes most effectively. One method would be to have the acolytes serve the elements in the pews after receiving them from the officiants. Another option is to have the acolytes serve as intermediaries, carrying elements from the altar or officiants to the ushers for distribution in the pews. Again, the possibilities are exciting and limited only by the pastor's tastes and creativity.

Acolytes should be allowed to commune at an appropriate time. They often receive the elements after the pastor and the assistant have communed and prior to the administration to the congregation.

Following the service, acolytes may assist the communion stewards in putting away the communion vessels, removing special paraments, and taking down banners.

The processional. In the church that has a processional cross, the acolyte designated as crucifer leads the worship leaders and choir in and out of the church while carrying the cross. (If there is no such cross, but the church does have a procession, acquiring a processional cross would enhance the worship experience for both acolytes and congregants; an escutcheon or banner may also be carried.) As the service begins, the crucifer processes into the chancel area, stands facing the altar while the other worship participants take their places, then puts the cross in its proper location. As with candlelighting, the crucifer reverses the order at the end of the service. Because of the significance and possible physical difficulty of this procedure, it is recommended that an older, taller acolyte be assigned this role. In addition, a full procession with flag bearers and banners will allow more acolytes to take an active part. Some churches have an acolyte carry in the Bible and place it on the lectern. It is important that all participants rehearse the processional to ensure correct pace and timing.

Baptism. During the service of baptism (by sprinkling), acolytes can be of real help to the pastor. They may stand on

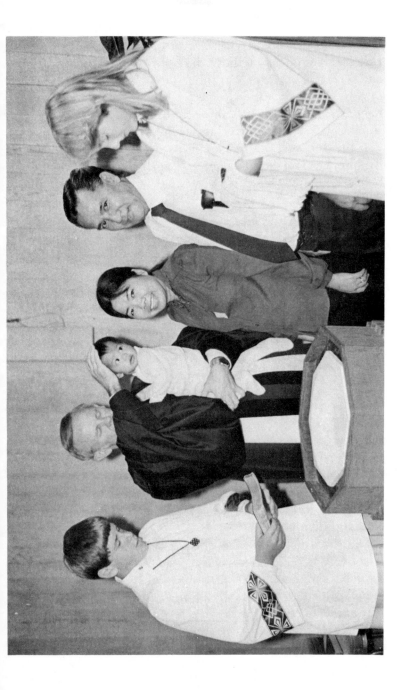

either side and slightly to the rear of the officiant during the ceremony. One may remove the cover from the baptismal font and replace it at the proper time. The other may hold the book of ritual and any certificates to be distributed, thus freeing the hands of the pastor. It is also helpful for the acolyte to carry a small towel on which the pastor may dry his or her hands.

If the method of immersion is used, acolytes may help with the preparation of garments and aid the pastor, as needed, before and after the immersion ritual.

Optional duties. Cleaning and polishing communion vessels; arranging altar cloths, paraments, and banners; and maintaining candles and wicks are all appropriate tasks for acolytes. The jobs of servicing the pews (placing envelopes, registration cards, and pencils in the racks; sharpening pencils; replacing hymnals and Bibles) and assisting the secretary in assembling bulletins, if needed, will provide youngsters with an opportunity to practice the stewardship of responsibility and service. Some churches also let acolytes change the announcements on the church marquee and signboards.

Special services. There are many ways for acolytes to participate in special services during the various seasons of the Christian year and on other special occasions. However, this should be done only if the participation of the acolytes will enhance the worship service. No special attention that distracts from the main theme of the worship service should center on them. Again, the acolytes must go about their tasks with quiet reverence and dignity.

One occasion in which additional acolytes may be used effectively is the Christmas Eve worship service. In one such service, I employed all available acolytes, fourteen in number. (This seemed an easier solution than choosing two and disappointing a dozen.) The service was a traditional candlelight communion with a great number of candles at various locations in the sanctuary, chancel, and nave. The acolytes took light for their candles from a Christ candle in the center of the altar (lighted prior to the prelude) and placed the lighted candles in holders on either side of the Christ candle. (The holders were hidden from the congregation by the Christmas decorations on the altar.) After the candles had been placed, the acolytes were seated in the front pews. Following the ritual for Holy Communion, the nave lights were turned off as the two acolytes who were assisting the pastor with communion lit candles (on candlestands) in the sanctuary. The elements were then administered to communicants by candlelight. When the communion service ended, all lights were turned off. The remaining candles in the chancel and nave were lit by other acolytes while the choir and congregation sang "Silent Night." The effect was profound! Never had there been more favorable comment on the beauty and meaningfulness of a worship service. The acolytes added greatly to that setting. They were very much in the spirit of the occasion, performing with quiet dignity and skill. It seemed to mean a great deal to each youngster to have a part, even a small part, in this most beautiful worship service of the year. A word of caution: The use of candles in great numbers can be a fire hazard, so the activity should be coordinated with local fire regulations.

Another occasion for using additional acolytes was Palm Sunday. Two acolytes were given palm branches to carry in the processional. They preceded the crucifer and, upon arrival at the altar, placed the branches in a prearranged spot. These became part of the Palm Sunday decorations for the sanctuary area. The church in which acolytes process with lighted tapers will need two additional acolytes for this service.

Mention should be made of acolytes at weddings. Unfortunately this is seldom done, since candles are usually lighted by ushers. The use of acolytes adds to the concept of the wedding as a service of worship and the acknowledgment of the spiritual presence of Christ. I have found that when acolytes are employed, their service is greatly appreciated. It will be up to the pastor or church wedding hostess to remind the bride and groom of the availability of acolytes.

There are many more opportunities for acolytes to be of service in the church. It is up to the pastor to utilize *creatively* this invaluable resource—the office of the acolyte.

VESTMENTS

Acolyte vestments usually consist of the standard cassock or a skirt (for both boys and girls) and cotta, which is a surplice or overgarment. The traditional cassock is black. However, colors can be used for the cassock or skirt, as well as decorative embroidery bands on the surplice to match the cassock. (One supply house lists the colors red, green, purple and gold.) The cassock should reach almost to the ankles, but not so long as to trip the acolyte. The cassock and surplice should be available in several sizes to accommodate variations in height and size. Skirts with adjustable hems are now available—a big advantage. Acolyte vestments should be hung neatly on hangers that are labeled clearly by size and/or name. A mother of one of the acolytes will be the ideal person to take responsibility for the robes. This "robe mother" may train the acolytes to hang their robes properly and give attention to keeping the robes neat and clean. She should check the robes frequently to determine what robes need to be laundered or repaired. It is especially important that the white surplice be laundered frequently so it will always look fresh and clean. There is little problem in maintaining the robes in churches that have designated an acolyte mother to coordinate the "keep the robes clean" project. Acolyte mothers are usually glad to do their share. "Acolyte fathers" may also perform these functions.

Where does one secure vestments for acolytes? If money is no object, the various robe companies or religious supply houses can provide them. However, many churches have relied on church members who sew. They can do excellent work, and patterns for the cassock and surplice are available from major pattern companies.

CHAPTER 3

Organizing the Acolytes

An organized acolyte program provides a unique learning experience and meaningful service opportunity for boys and girls. Just as important as instruction and service is the discipline the program affords a busy pastor to be committed to regular periods of involvement with youngsters in their impressionable years. The structure and type of program will vary with the size of the church, the interest of the pastor, and the time and opportunity available. The following outline can be adapted to each local situation.

A. RECRUITMENT AND REQUIREMENTS

Where does one find candidates for the acolyte program? The church school classes and the youth groups (if older acolytes are used) are two obvious sources. Church school teachers and counselors may recommend candidates, but best results occur when the pastor visits the classes, preferably in early fall, to explain and promote the acolyte program. Before leaving the classroom the pastor can get some indication of the number of young people interested. The teacher may be asked to follow through and supply a list of those prospects. Then a letter of invitation may be mailed to the children and their parents.* Once a successful program is under way, there may be more candidates than can be handled. After a program is established, the youth in the program will recruit brothers, sisters, and friends, and eventually a simple announcement in the church newsletter and bulletin is sufficient to fill the class. The program sells itself.

What ages should be considered for the acolyte program? This is a determination each pastor must make. Of major consideration is the extent and purpose of the local program. If lighting candles on Sundays is the only goal, then ages nine to nineteen are acceptable. But if a group is formed for purposes of education, fellowship, and spiritual development, then consideration should be given to age-grouping. From much experience, I have found that the ages of nine to twelve inclusive are best for a comprehensive acolyte program for the aforementioned purposes. A wide age-span complicates instruction and fellowship.

It is important to establish standards of qualification in the acolyte program. Regular attendance at training sessions and passing tests on relevant materials is basic. As an example, one church requires the students to pass three tests and thoroughly rehearse all worship procedures before assuming the role of acolytes. Details will be discussed in the next chapter.

B. RECOGNITION

When the class has reached the designated point in the "basic training" schedule, there should be a service of installation (see Appendix 7). Significance will be added to this event by presenting the acolytes with some symbol of achievement and identity, such as a small gold-plated acolyte pin. In one church, after a year of faithful service, a small silver cross is

---

*The letter may be in the form of a nomination from the pastor and/or the committee on worship.

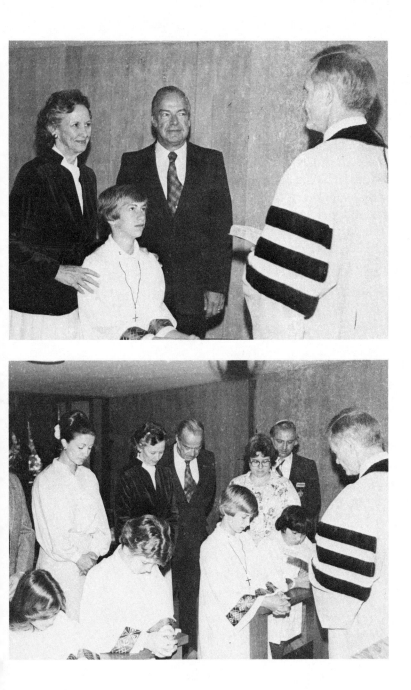

presented to those who qualify. The cross is suspended by a black cord suitable for wearing around the neck over the acolyte vestments. In another church, the acolyte is given a wooden cross to wear around the neck. After a year's probation, the wooden cross is replaced by a silver-plated cross, on the back of which is engraved the name of the acolyte and the year. The acolytes wear their crosses hung over a wide cross-shaped ribbon in the appropriate seasonal color. Some churches utilize a different symbol for each year of service. For example, after the first year the acolyte receives a pin; second year, a silver cross; third year, a Jerusalem cross; and fourth year, an elaborate medallion depicting the altar with a chalice, loaf of bread, and candles.*

C. ROSTER AND SCHEDULING

The number of acolytes who can be accommodated in the church's program should be considered. Regular opportunities to serve in the Sunday worship service are important in maintaining enthusiasm. If a church has only one Sunday service, twelve acolytes is a good number to work with. If three acolytes are used for the service, each youth can serve at least once a month. The number can be expanded if there are several services each Sunday. A schedule should be set up for at least three months in advance and mailed to each home. This will allow necessary changes to be made to suit each family's calendar. The schedule should also include such special services as Thanksgiving, Christmas Eve, Maundy Thursday. The church secretary or one of the acolyte parents could be responsible for making out the schedule. Consideration should be given to the height of the acolytes in teaming them together. Also, the older (or larger) of the three in a team might be listed as "crucifer." A copy of the schedule should be

*Medallion manufactured by Terra Sancta Guild, available from religious supply houses.

available at all times in the church office, and the Sunday bulletin may list the names of the acolytes serving that Sunday, along with those of the choir director, ushers, and so on.

D. REGULAR MEETINGS

In conducting a comprehensive acolyte program, it is important that regular meeting times be established, avoiding church calendar conflicts. Each time period can be utilized to accomplish the following: (1) instruction and training, (2) carrying out routine service projects, (3) group devotions and business, and (4) recreation. If the group is large enough, officers may be elected and a simple constitution and bylaws could be established, clearly setting forth the purpose and goals. In one church I served, a regular Saturday morning schedule was followed. It ran something like this:

9:30   Acolytes begin to arrive for service projects, such as folding bulletins in the church office and servicing pews in the nave

10:15   Meeting called to order by president of acolytes; prayer by pastor, adult worker, or older acolyte; business session; training and/or instruction period (or testing if applicable)

11:00   Recreation and/or refreshments

When the program includes ten or more acolytes, it is essential that the pastor have an assistant at each meeting.

Many churches conduct the acolyte training program on weekdays after school. Some of these programs are only one hour long and are used primarily for training and instruction. It is recommended that refreshments and a brief recreation period be included. The following is a suggested timetable:

3:30   Refreshments available for the youth as they arrive from school

3:45   Instruction/test period by pastor
4:00   Acolyte rehearsal in sanctuary
4:30   Closing prayer circle

Note: After the acolytes have been enrolled, a list of the class members with addresses and phone numbers should be given to each acolyte parent. This will be useful in organizing car pools and assigning refreshment responsibilities for each week.

E. EXTRA ACTIVITIES

Group morale and interest will blossom when field trips, retreats, and the like are included in the yearly programming. These events allow additional opportunity for the pastor to relate meaningfully to these youngsters. If your church building is not one of traditional architecture (such as the cruciform), it would be advantageous to visit such a church. This could serve as a primary model for the suggested lesson in chapter 4, "Training the Acolytes." Trips to ball games or the beach with the children and their parent(s), hiking, and picnics should be planned. Weekend retreats for acolytes and their parent(s) are also rewarding experiences. The youngsters are usually most anxious to cooperate in helping finance such adventures by collecting dues and engaging in minor fund-raising projects.

CHAPTER 4

Training the Acolytes

When the pastor undertakes a serious training program for acolytes, the natural next step is confirmation and membership preparation. Acolyte training should supplement, not duplicate, the existing church school or membership preparation curriculum. The possibilities are exciting.

COURSE OF INSTRUCTION

The following curriculum outline is one model, but each leader is encouraged to develop his or her own ideas.

Session 1: The office of acolyte. History of and qualifications for the office. Acolyte Code of Conduct (see page 34). Responsibilities and duties of acolytes (see Appendix 1). Overview of the acolyte program and schedule of classes.

Session 2: Significance of Christian architecture and the traditional church. Learning the technical names for the parts of the church (see Appendix 2).

Session 3: Christian symbolism, with particular reference to symbols found in the acolytes' own church building. For resources, refer to booklets on symbolism (see Appendix 3).

Session 4: Seasons and colors of the Christian calendar (see Appendix 4).

Session 5: Explanation of the Order of Worship and use of the Sunday bulletin (see Appendix 5).

Session 6: Hymnody. Use of the hymnbook and ritual (see Appendix 6).

Session 7: The life of Christ, a brief history of the church, and the meaning of Christian discipleship. Adapt denominational doctrinal statements to make a catechism that will include basic material on these topics.

For these sessions, use materials available from your denominational curriculum. If none is available or suitable, prepare your own. If permitted, duplicate adapted material for use by the class. Provide each student with an inexpensive folder in which to keep the various materials of the course.

TESTING

Simple, objective tests (see Appendixes 2, 3 and 4) are given on material presented in the second, third, and fourth sessions. The same could be done for the other sessions, too. During the session on the "catechism," the dialogue method provides an ideal opportunity for the pastor to relate to the youngsters on a personal level and explore with them basic Christian tenets.

QUALIFICATION

A policy needs to be established on when and how one "qualifies" to make his or her debut as an acolyte in the worship service (see Appendix 1). It is recommended that this not happen until at least half the studies have been completed and tests have been passed. For example, the policy might state that no one may serve as acolyte in the service of worship until he or she has passed the first three tests and has thoroughly rehearsed the procedures for the worship services. Make sure all students understand the policy when they are first recruited.

MINI-WORSHIP REHEARSAL

The happiest discovery I have made in the years of working with acolytes is the rewarding and fun "mini-worship rehearsal." Parts of the worship service are recreated by using the acolytes to light the candles, assist with the offering, assist with a baptism, and sing the opening and closing hymns. While the boys and girls are rehearsing two at a time as acolytes, the others in the class are playing roles of the pastor, choir director, ushers, liturgist, organist, and congregation. And they love it! The enthusiasm displayed easily becomes an effective tool for learning the rudiments of the worship service as well as the duties of acolyting. By the time everyone has had the opportunity to play the various roles, much has been learned about the elements of worship and its leadership. The youth gain basic insights into the corporate worship experience. If the organist or another musician is available to play some of the hymns and musical responses during the mini-service, the experience will be enhanced. If not, a tape recording of the musical parts of the service may be useful.

Prior to these rehearsals, the acolytes should be taught certain basics, such as keeping step, which promotes dignity and neatness. Walking should be done slowly and naturally. Another basic is coordinating all actions so that everything is done together. Being deliberate in all movements will help here. For example, when lighting the candles, both acolytes should make sure the other acolyte's candle is lit before removing his or her own candlelighter, so it can be done together. The acolytes can be trained to anticipate each other's moves when starting, stopping, and turning. It is a good idea from the beginning to teach reverence for the sanctuary/altar area and cross. Insist on proper decorum, even during rehearsals.

CONDUCT IN THE CHURCH BUILDING

From the very beginning of the program, the acolytes should be taught appropriate manners and attire while in the church facility. It is helpful to give frequent reminders of that behavior in a positive manner. Otherwise the pastor and assistant will find themselves constantly repeating, after the fact, "Don't do that, John!" The leader may enlist the aid of the boys and girls in setting up an "Acolyte Code of Conduct." The following may serve as a model:

Acolyte Code of Conduct

1. The worship area of the church must be respected with reverence. This includes the occasions when you are rehearsing or servicing pews, as well as during mini-worship services. Walk, do not run, to your appointed tasks when indoors, and always remove hats or caps.

2. Acolytes remember that good grooming is important for anyone in public worship services. Make sure you have clean hands, clean fingernails, clean shoes, combed hair, and appropriate clothing.

3. Acolytes can be very helpful in assisting the pastor to begin each worship service on time by being present at least twenty minutes before the service is to begin. This will allow time to get robed, check the tapers in the candlelighter, and receive any last-minute instructions from the pastor.

34

4. Since anything that calls undue attention to self during worship is out of place, acolytes are always careful not to distract worshipers. Acolytes set the example as the pastor's helpers, and know that to chew gum, whisper, or sit improperly in the pew is distracting and therefore out of place.

5. In lighting the candlelighters, acolytes should be sure to receive assistance from the ushers or other adults. Never leave matches accessible to others.

PREPARATION FOR THE WORSHIP SERVICE

To help the acolytes feel the importance of their position and their responsibility in worship, include them in the period of prayer before the service with the pastor, liturgist, and choir. You may provide a simple prayer for the acolytes to learn and to pray in unison, such as:

Our God, we thank you for the privilege of serving you and your church. Increase in us reverence and humility, that our participation may assist all who gather for worship. In the name of Christ. Amen.

ACOLYTE PROGRAM FOR THE SECOND YEAR AND BEYOND

The program for acolytes can continue indefinitely beyond the initial basic training. Successful programs have been set up for acolytes in the second, third, and fourth years, using an advanced curriculum. Various suitable resources for continued acolyte training and instruction are available. Church school materials could, of course, be adapted. Some acolyte programs have used the booklets from Channing L. Bete Co.,

Inc.,* such as "About Christianity," "ABC's of World Religions," "The Bible and You," and the different denominational booklets.

In this multi-age program, additional staff is needed to handle the two or more classes. At least one church is known to have from forty to fifty acolytes in a weekday training experience that served as the church's weekday Christian education program.

AFTER ACOLYTES—THEN WHAT?

What happens to those who "graduate" from the acolyte program either because of passing the age limit or disinterest? It behooves the pastor and/or worship committee to provide other opportunities for them. Former acolytes could serve well on the altar guild, assisting in the care of the sanctuary, the paraments, communion trays, and so on. Others could serve as ushers, and some could assist in the church school. The church must create opportunities for youth to continue the church service career that began with the acolyte program. Their commitment, made at an early age, should be allowed expression in other areas and at all age levels, particularly the "awkward" ecclesiastical years of the teenager.

In reality the acolyte program never ends, for one does not graduate from the commission to be a *follower* of Christ and a *helper* of other people. If the Christian's pilgrimage were to be described in terms of a book, an early chapter might well be titled "Acolyte Training." Church membership involves lifelong training in Christian discipleship, and the acolyte program is an excellent tool for practicing these disciplines at an early age.

In my first pastorate I started using acolytes even though I had no previous experience and did not inherit a ready-made

---

*Channing L. Bete Co., Inc. 200 State Road, South Deerfield, MA 01373

program. My first acolytes were youngsters from ten to fifteen years old. No age requirements or other qualifications had been established. After the program was under way, other youngsters expressed interest in participating. I shall never forget one cute, pudgy boy of eight named Johnny. He wanted very much to be an acolyte, but he was too short to reach the altar candles even with the candlelighter. Nevertheless, he would look at me with big brown eyes and a charming smile and ask, "Can I light the candles on Sunday?" or "When can I be an ak-lite?" I was able to put him off with the promise, "When you are able to reach the candles, you may become an acolyte." That seemed to satisfy him. Thereafter I frequently observed little Johnny in the sanctuary with candlelighter in hand, straining on his tiptoes to reach the candlewicks. This continued for several months. Then one day, as I sat in my study, I heard the sound of little running feet. Like a ray of sunlight bursting through the clouds, in came Johnny, all aglow. I knew what had happened. "Guess what, Pastor?" Without waiting for my response, he blurted, "I can be an ak-lite now! I can reach, I can reach it!" Sure enough, his stretching and straining had been rewarded. Not only had he reached the candles, he had reached a new plateau in his life! Little Johnny became one of the very best acolytes I've ever known, and I've often recalled how he stretched to reach his goal. He was sincere, enthusiastic, and committed. Through the acolyte program he found a channel for expressing the Christian's response to Christ's call at an early age. A comprehensive acolyte program will provide an ideal way for other Johnnys and Janes to stretch their young spiritual muscles as *followers* of Christ and reach an important stage in Christian discipleship.

Appendixes

(Materials in the appendixes are intended as aids in preparing for the training sessions and the final installation service. Suggested sessions for using the material are indicated.)

APPENDIX 1

General Procedures for Acolytes
(*Session 1*)

The following is a sample of a notice that might be sent home to parents at the first session with the new acolyte class.

GENERAL PROCEDURES FOR ACOLYTES

In order to fulfill the proper function as an acolyte, there are certain duties involved with this honored and privileged position.

Acolyte Training Course

1. Each acolyte should complete a training course conducted by the pastor. This will include five or more lessons held each Wednesday afternoon from 3:30 to 4:30. Acolytes will be rehearsed on procedures for worship services: lighting candles, assisting with communion and baptism, and other duties.

2. An acolyte will be eligible for participation in Sunday worship services after the first three tests are taken and passed.

3. At the close of the class, acolytes will be consecrated (along with their parents) on Acolyte Recognition Sunday, which

will be scheduled for later in the church year. Each acolyte will receive a gold-plated acolyte pin.

4. Acolytes may elect officers and have brief business sessions at each meeting.

5. Parents will be asked to provide refreshments for the class on a rotating basis.

Duties of Acolytes

1. When a youth qualifies to serve as an acolyte, he or she will be scheduled for a three-month period, and a schedule will be sent home. Please check the schedule with your family calendar, and if your scheduled Sunday conflicts, you should (a) secure a replacement by contacting one of the other acolytes, or (b) notify the office in time to secure a substitute and put the information in the bulletin. Each acolyte should know his or her schedule.

2. On the Sunday he or she serves, each acolyte should wear a white shirt or blouse, dark pants or skirt, and make sure shoes are clean. Black shoes are preferred, but conservative dress shoes may be worn.

3. Acolytes should arrive about 20 minutes before the start of the service and (a) get robed; (b) check the wicks on candle-lighters, making sure there is enough wick for the service.

4. It shall be the duty of the acolyte to assist in preparing for the Sunday worship services. This may include servicing the sanctuary and church grounds.

APPENDIX 2

Architecture and the Traditional Church (*Session 2*)

Church architecture is a subject that will enable the acolytes to feel at home in the church building and appreciate its physical significance. It also provides the opportunity to learn some of the basics of Christian worship and theology, and a little church history as well. If possible, provide some visual aids (books, filmstrips, literature) that depict architectural variety.* What type of architecture is represented by the acolytes' home church? If possible, have available resources showing the development of Christian architecture from Solomon's temple up to the cruciform (cross-shaped) church. At some point in the program, a field trip to several churches and a Jewish synagogue will be an enriching experience. It is especially important to visit a cross-shaped church if the home church is not of this design.

If your church facility is more modern, this instruction period may take the form of an imaginary visit to a "traditional church." It might begin by explaining the three major parts of the church building: the nave, the chancel, and the sanctuary.

---

*A book showing a large variety of recent church architecture is *Tradition Becomes Innovation: Modern Religious Architecture in America* by Bartlett Hayes (New York: The Pilgrim Press, 1983). $12.95 (paper).

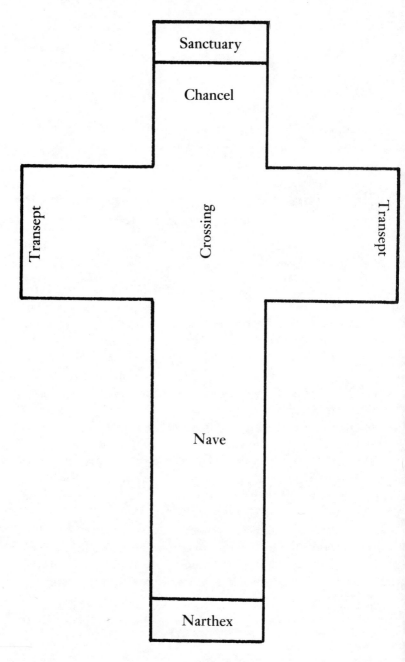

42

The nave is the largest area, where the people sit. If the church has gothic-like beams, a simple illustration will enable the boys and girls readily to remember the nave. Tell them to think of the beams above them as the ribs of a ship's hull upside down. The navy has ships. The word nave sounds like navy (same root word). Also remind them that the church has often been referred to as the "ship of faith."

The chancel area is where the pulpit, lectern, and choir stalls are located. The lectern is where the Bible is placed for reading.

The transepts represent the arms of the cross and separate the nave and the chancel. In early church history, the transepts were occupied by clergy and acolytes.

Beyond the chancel is the sanctuary, or altar area. The kneeling rail separates the chancel and the sanctuary. Here the people kneel to pray and receive communion. The altar symbolizes the throne of God and during communion may serve as the Lord's Table. The altar area is reminiscent of the ancient holy of holies, such as that found in Solomon's temple. Its position in the traditional church indicates that God is the center of our worship and that the entire service is directed toward God.

The different parts of the church have symbolic meaning too. The nave represents the church in this world; the chancel, the church expectant (or those who have passed into the life beyond). In many European churches, saints lie buried beneath the chancel area. The sanctuary represents the church triumphant (or the church at the end of the age, when Christ shall reign).

And what of the long aisle? It is symbolic of the journey through life from birth (traditionally locating the baptismal font in the narthex, which symbolized baptism as the first step into new life) to death and leading finally to the presence of God. The steps leading upward from the nave to the altar recall that the journey through life should be an upward one. Usually, there would be seven steps in all, three of which would lead from the chancel to the altar. Seven is thought of as a complete number in the Bible. Three symbolizes the Trinity—"Father, Son, and Holy Spirit."

Other symbolism may be pointed out, for example, the vigil light recognizing the eternal vigilance of the church and God's care, the stained-glass windows rich in symbolism, the carvings, and even the church bell, which proclaims God's priority in our lives.

There is a potential bonus here. Many people are unaware of the rich symbolism of their own church buildings. The acolyte program will help make them all more appreciative of those symbolic features and thus enrich their worship experience.

ACOLYTE QUIZ: ARCHITECTURE AND THE TRADITIONAL CHURCH*

Date_____   Name_____
Score_____   Grade_____

True and False (Circle T if statement is true, F if false.)

1. T F   The nave represents the church at work or moving forward.

2. T F   The altar symbolizes the throne of God.

3. T F   The traditional church building has three parts.

4. T F   The baptismal font was located in the narthex in traditional church buildings.

5. T F   The transepts (arms of the cross) are where clergy and acolytes were seated.

---

*This quiz may be reproduced for educational purposes in the local church. The copyright notice on page 4 should appear on the first page of all copies of the quiz.

Matching (In the blank next to the words below, put the number of the description that matches.)

1. Where the congregation sits

2. The area occupied by the minister and choir

3. The area in which the altar stands

4. Representing the three natures of God: "Father, Son, and Holy Spirit"

5. Between the chancel and the nave, a place to kneel for prayer and to receive communion

6. Where the Bible is placed for the reading of the holy scriptures

7. Podium for preaching

a. Three____   e. Sanctuary____

b. Lectern____   f. Kneeling (communion) rail____

c. Nave____   g. Chancel____

d. Pulpit____

APPENDIX 3

Christian Symbols
(*Session 3*)

In the session on Christian symbols, a good book on symbols will be a valuable aid,* as will filmstrips, charts, and so on. If you have artists in your congregation, they can draw several basic symbols that can be duplicated on a sheet with brief explanations for study by the class. If your church building has stained-glass windows and other areas where Christian symbols are found, these can also be included. Here is a sampling of symbols, followed by a quiz:

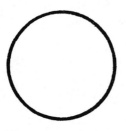

The circle with its unending line represents the eternal nature of God.

Our Christian Symbols by Friedrich Rest (New York: The Pilgrim Press, 1954) is widely used.

The Latin cross is the best known of the more than fifty forms of the cross and symbolizes the crucifixion and Christ.

The Easter lily, which is "reborn" annually from its bulb, represents the resurrection and the Christian's hope of immortality.

The fish was a secret sign used by early Christians to identify themselves during the period of persecution by Roman police. The fish was chosen because its spelling in Greek uses the first letters for the words "Jesus Christ Son of God Savior."

IHS

These first three letters in the Greek word for Jesus frequently appear on altars and other church furnishings.

The candle is used to represent Jesus, the light of the world.

These Greek letters, alpha and omega, are the first and last letters of the Greek alphabet and call to mind Jesus' words, "I am the Alpha and Omega, the beginning and the end."

The triangle represents the Trinity, the threefold nature of God: God the "Father, Son, and Holy Spirit."

The Creator's Star formed of two triangles represents the attributes of God: power, wisdom, majesty, love, mercy, and justice.

The chi (X) and rho (P), letters from the Greek word for Christ, are often shown superimposed to serve as a symbol of Jesus. It is pronounced khy (like why) rō.

ACOLYTE QUIZ: SYMBOLISM*

Date_____ Name_____
Score_____ Grade_____

True and False (Circle T if statement is true, F if false.)

1. T F   The circle in Christian symbolism represents the eternal nature of God.

2. T F   There are more than fifty forms of crosses, the best known being the Latin cross.

3. T F   The Easter lily is symbolic of the beauty of the church.

4. T F   The fish was used by the persecuted Christians to convey a message to other Christians without the message being understood by the Roman police.

Matching (In the blank next to the words below, put the number of the description that matches.)

    a. The light of the world (Jesus)

    b. The beginning and the end

    c. Greek letters representing Jesus

    d. The Trinity—"Father, Son and Holy Spirit"

1. Triangle____   3. Candle____

2. Alpha and Omega____   4. Chi-Rho

The Creator's Star has two triangles, making six points. The six points are said to refer to the attributes of God. Name four of those six attributes.

1. _____   3. _____

2. _____   4. _____

What do the letters "IHS" stand for?

_____

APPENDIX 4

Church Seasons and Colors
(*Session 4*)

SEASONS OF THE CHRISTIAN YEAR

The seasons of the Christian year and their accompanying themes teach and recall the events in the life of Christ and the great traditions and emphases of the faith.

It should be pointed out that the events commemorated throughout the church year did not necessarily occur on the same dates as the contemporary celebrations of them. The important fact is that there is a calendar which provides for an orderly observance of the great events of the faith in order to intensify and further beliefs.

The seasons parallel nature to a marked degree. Christmas comes at that time of year when one looks forward to more hours of daylight. The shortest day in the year has been passed. Easter roughly coincides with the planting time, and Kingdomtide with the long growing and maturing time. By Advent Sunday, the harvest has been gathered, and Christians prepare their minds for another year of growth and development in Christ.

Advent. The first Sunday in Advent is the Sunday nearest November 30. The Advent season continues until Christmas

Eve. The word advent comes from the Latin *adventus* meaning "coming" or "arrival." For hundreds of years before Christ came, the priests and prophets of ancient Israel predicted his coming and sought to prepare the hearts of the people for his arrival. Modern Christians need all of the advent season to prepare their hearts for the great fact that Christmas celebrates.

Christmastide. Beginning with Christmas Day, this season lasts until January 5 and is followed by the festival of the Epiphany.

The Epiphany. The Epiphany occurs on January 6, and its season has from one to six Sundays, depending on the date of Easter. It is the season that celebrates Christ's manifestation to the Magi (Wise Men) and the gentile world. Pre-Lent (Gesima) within Epiphany makes us mindful of approaching Ash Wednesday.

Lent. The term Lent means "long days" or "Spring." To most church members, Lent is associated with a time of fasting and penitence in preparation for Easter. Lent recalls Jesus' forty-day vigil in the wilderness in preparation for his ministry. It begins with Ash Wednesday, a name derived from the ancient custom of burning the palms that had been blessed on Palm Sunday of the previous year. The ashes were then placed on the foreheads of the faithful in the form of a cross. It is interesting to note that the six Sundays of Lent are not part of Lent. Each Sunday commemorates Easter and is a respite from fasting.

Easter. Easter has always been the climactic festival of the Christian year as it celebrates Jesus' resurrection. It is the point around which the rest of the church year revolves. Because Easter Day is always the first Sunday following the first full moon after the Spring equinox it may occur anywhere between March 22 and April 25. Eastertide is a season of forty days ending with Ascension Day. Its central theme is renewal and hope for the future.

Pentecost (or Whitsuntide). Pentecost is frequently called the birthday of the Christian church. The Holy Spirit was poured out to the apostles fifty days after Easter while they were gathered in the upper room. Because new converts in the early church were baptized in white garments, the term White Sunday, and later Whitsunday, was used. Pentecost literally means "the fiftieth day." This season lasts one week, leading to Trinity Sunday.

Kingdomtide. Kingdomtide completes the cycle begun with Advent. The word growth seems to sum up best the purpose of this approximately three-month-long season, offering the church opportunities for stressing the practical side of Christian life as the necessary fruit of the Christian faith. Kingdomtide emphases include the spiritual nature of Christ's kingdom and the social implications of the gospel, such as the Sermon on the Mount, the Lord's Prayer, and the kingdom parables. Kingdomtide is a term coined to stress Jesus' ideal of the kingdom of God on earth. It always begins with the last Sunday of August and continues through the Sunday before Advent.

THE CHURCH (ECCLESIASTICAL) COLORS

Color is often a vehicle to express meaning. The use of colors in the church's furnishings (paraments, banners, etc.) is a way of symbolizing theological truths for the people.

Purple signifies royalty (Jesus as the King of kings), penitence, and discipline. Used during Advent and Lent.

Green signifies nature, growth, and life and is the color designated for Epiphany and Kingdomtide (or Trinity).

Red symbolizes blood, fire, and Christian zeal. It is used for the short season of Pentecost and Whitsuntide and on Reformation and Thanksgiving days.

White is the color of purity, chastity, light, and rejoicing, and is the color appropriate for Easter Day and Eastertide, Christmas Day and Christmastide.

Black, the color of mourning, is used only on Good Friday, to recall Christ's suffering.

ACOLYTE QUIZ: SEASONS AND COLORS*

Date_____   Name_____
Score_____   Grade_____

True and False (Circle T if statement is true, F if false.)

1. T   F   The word advent comes from the Latin *adventus*, meaning "coming" or "arrival."

2. T   F   The seasons of the church year are to be learned only by ministers and acolytes.

3. T   F   The season of Epiphany marks the beginning of the Christmas season.

4. T   F   White Sunday (Whitsunday) relates to the baptism of converts who were robed in white.

5. T   F   The six Sundays of Lent are not part of Lent.

Matching   (In the blank next to the words below, put the number of the description that matches.)

1. Means "long days" or "Spring." A period of forty days of fasting and penitence in preparation for Easter.

2. Takes its name from the ancient custom of burning palms that had been blessed on Palm Sunday the previous year. The ashes were placed on the foreheads of the faithful in the form of a cross.

---

*This quiz may be reproduced for educational purposes in the local church. The copyright notice on page **4** should appear on the first page of all copies of the quiz.

3. The "birthday" of the Christian church.

4. The longest season of the church year.

    a. Kingdomtide____   c. Pentecost____

    b. Lent____   d. Ash Wednesday____

Put the following in order by number

__1__ Advent   ____ Epiphany   ____ Christmas

____ Trinity   ____Lent   ____ Easter

What are the church colors for the following?

Easter_____   • Christmas_____

Lent_____   Kingdomtide or

Whitsuntide_____   Trinity Season_____

APPENDIX 5

Explanation of Worship Order (*Session 5*)

Perhaps using the scripture passage Isaiah 6:1–8 as a basis, give a theological explanation for the sequence of worship events. (Follow the worship bulletin for your church.) The order has been described as similar to a drama, with God as the audience, the pastor and the other leaders as "prompters," and the congregation as actors. The acronym ACTED is also helpful in describing the flow of the service from Adoration, Confession, Thanksgiving, Education, to Dedication. Point out the types of prayers and hymns appropriate for those parts of the service. A theological understanding of the nature and sequence of worship will be of major benefit to the acolytes.

APPENDIX 6

The Hymnal and Book of Worship
(*Session 6*)

The hymnal (and book of worship, if used in your church) is an excellent source for instruction on the nature of worship and ritual. After passing out a copy to each acolyte, begin thumbing through the hymnbook, commenting on the contents and how the hymnal may be used. The preface might contain interesting material on how the book was prepared. Draw attention to the way in which hymns are categorized according to theme, ecclesiastical season, and scriptural references. Familiarize the acolytes with the types of indexes available. If orders of worship and specific rituals are included, look at them briefly. As part of the lesson on worship, the acolytes might benefit from gathering in small groups to plan a service on a certain theme, making use of the hymnal in the process.

APPENDIX 7

Installation Service for Acolytes

(The acolytes assemble at the chancel rail with parents standing behind them.)

Pastor: We are gathered to install these young people as acolytes, a significant ministry in the history of the church. The title acolyte is derived from the Greek word meaning to follow, serve, or assist. It is an ancient office dating back to the earliest days of the Christian faith. It is an office, then, to be entered into with commitment and respect.

Pastor to acolytes: You who stand here today have been carefully trained in your duties and taught the significance of your responsibilities. Will you strive to conduct yourselves reverently and responsibly in this role of service to the church and devotion to God?

Response: We will.

Pastor: Long ago when acolytes were ordained by the church, during the ceremony of ordination the bishop presented each acolyte with a candle to symbolize that the church would be in the acolyte's care. The tradition continued long after acolytes ceased to be ordained. At their installation or dedication, candles were presented to them in recognition of their principal duty of lighting the candles on the altar. *(To acolytes:)* I now give each of you a candle representing the sacred and honorable tradition of the office of acolyte.

(The pastor or veteran acolytes distribute candles to the new acolytes, who file to the altar to receive light from the Christ candles, then place the lit candles in a waiting candelabrum. A variation might be to have the pastor bring a light from the altar flame and light each youngster's candle, after which the acolytes place their candles in separate waiting candlesticks on the altar or in a special place.)

Pastor to parents: These young people are assuming a major role in the life of this congregation. They will need your help in meeting their responsibilities. Will you renew your dedication to this church by promising to give them encouragement and assistance in fulfilling these important tasks?

Response: We will.

Pastor to congregation: I present to you now these people who desire to serve the church in the ministry of acolytes. *(Read the names.)* Will you accept them, support them in their role, and rededicate yourselves to the high calling of worship to the glory of God?

Response: We will.

(The pastor presents each acolyte with a pin or other item of commemoration and gives a word of blessing to each.)

Pastor: Let us pray.

Congregation: (Print prayer in bulletin.) O God, we come before you in humility to ask your blessings on our corporate acts of worship. Increase our sense of your presence, guide our response to your calling, and strengthen our resolve to serve you and your people. In the name of Jesus Christ our Lord. Amen.